PIANO

Adventures®

Arranged by Nancy and Randall Faber
THE BASIC PIANO METHOD

Production Coordinator: Jon Ophoff
Cover and Illustration: Terpstra Design, San Francisco
Engraving: Dovetree Productions, Inc.

FABER
PIANO ADVENTURES®
3042 Creek Drive
Ann Arbor, Michigan 48108

ISBN 978-1-61677-260-4

A Note to Teacher and Parents

For decades, popular repertoire has captured the hearts of people worldwide. Perhaps it is the memorable melodies, engaging lyrics, and catchy rhythms that create its magic and universal appeal. Some of America's finest music makers have left us a legacy that will be treasured for all time—Henry Mancini's *The Pink Panther*; Julie Gold's *From a Distance*; and Peter Yarrow and Leonard Lipton's *Puff, The Magic Dragon*.

Piano Adventures® Popular Repertoire (Level 3A) offers a unique teaching experience for teacher and student alike. Outstanding popular repertoire has been skillfully arranged and correlated with the concepts in the Piano Adventures® Lesson Book (Level 3A). A notable feature of *Piano Adventures® Popular Repertoire* is the fun-filled activity page that follows each popular selection. At Level 3A, these pages imaginatively engage the student in harmony, ear training, rhythmic study, sightreading, and the understanding of musical terms. A music dictionary at the end of the book provides a quick and easy reference for basic musical terms.

So have fun! America's finest popular repertoire has now been pedagogically presented with what many are calling the finest method ever—*Piano Adventures®*!

FF1260

C O N T E N T S

Puff, The Magic Dragon

Words and Music by
Peter Yarrow and Leonard Lipton

Moderately

(R.H. 8va on verses 2 and 4)

Puff the Mag - ic Drag - on lived by the
geth - er they would trav - el on a boat with bil - lowed

sea, and frol - icked in the au - tumn mist in a
sail. Jack - ie kept a look - out perched on

land called Hon - a - lee. Lit - tle Jack - ie
Puff's gi - gan - tic tail. Nob - le kings and

Pa - per loved that ras - cal, Puff, and
princ - es bow when 'er they came.

FF1260

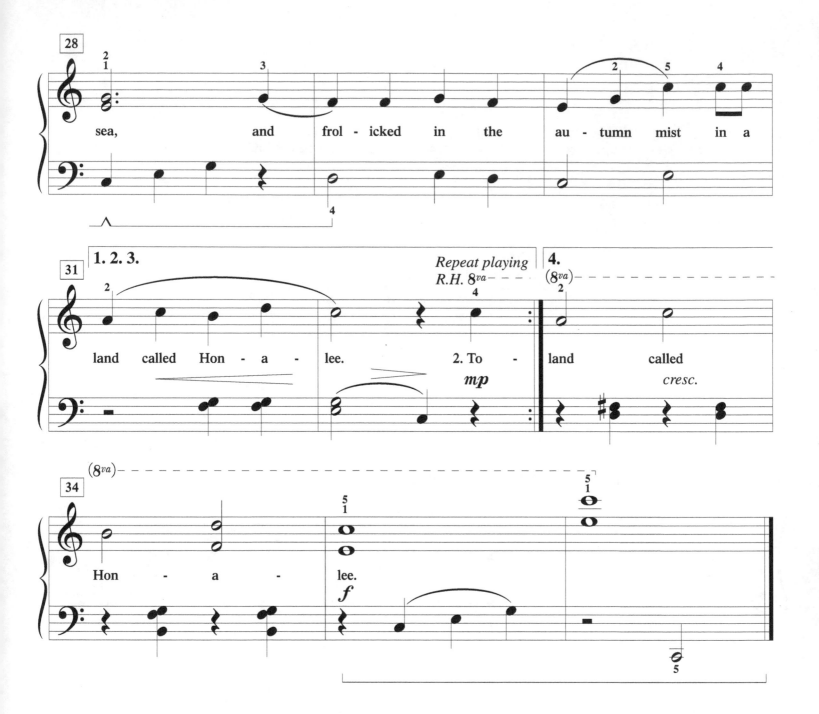

Additional Lyrics

3. A dragon lives forever, but not so little boys,
   Painted wings and giant rings make way for other toys.
   One gray night it happened, Jackie Paper came no more,
   And Puff that mighty dragon, he ceased his fearless roar. Oh! *To Chorus*

4. His head was bent in sorrow, green tears fell like rain;
   Puff no longer went to play along the cherry lane.
   Without his life-long friend, Puff could not be brave,
   So Puff that mighty dragon, sadly slipped into his cave. *To Chorus*

How is the music different when the opening measures return at *measure 17*?

Variations on a Dragon Theme

- Write the **chord symbol** for each measure in the box given.
  - *major chord* = capital letter (Ex. **C**)
  - *minor chord* = capital letter plus lowercase "m" (Ex. **Em**)

- Sightread each example at a s-l-o-w tempo. Use pedal.
  - Reading the chord symbols will help you find the L.H. notes quickly.

Puff, The Magic Dragon

Words and Music by
Peter Yarrow and Leonard Lipton

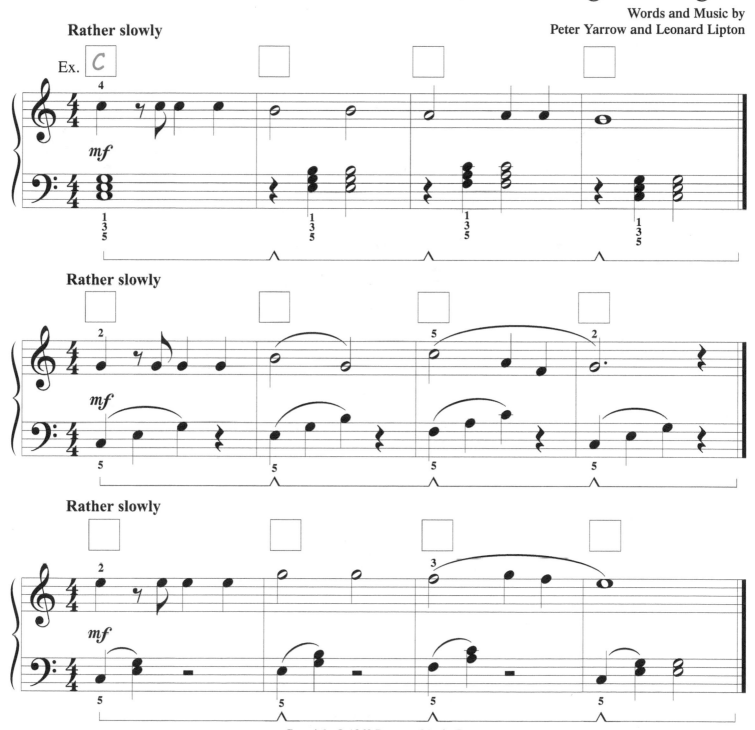

¢ Cut Time = $\frac{2}{2}$

Cut time is $\frac{4}{4}$ time divided by half: $\frac{2}{2}$

It is notated the same as $\frac{4}{4}$ time, but is played with **2 beats per measure**.

The ♩ receives one beat.

Tiny Toon Adventures
(Theme Song)

Lyrics by
**Wayne Kaatz, Tom Ruegger,
and Bruce Broughton**

Music by
Bruce Broughton

We're ti - ny, we're toon - ey, we're all a lit - tle loon - ey, and this af - ter - noon - y we're in - vad - ing your T. V. We're

FF1260

FF1260

"We're looney, we're tooney. . ."

Answer the musical question coming from each "looney" character.

1. Say, kiddo, what does **cut time** mean?

$\mathbf{2 \atop 2}$ means ___ beats per measure

means the ___ note receives the beat

2. *Tsk! Tsk!* Can you circle the two chords used in *measures 5–10*?

IV and **V7**   **I** and **IV**   **I** and **V7**

3. "Put your thinking cap on, wise guy!" In which two measures does the R.H. use a "snatch" of the **chromatic scale**?

measure_____ and *measure _____*

4. "Keep you peepers open! It's no accident to use an *accidental*."

Can you name a **sharp**, **flat**, and **natural** used in this piece?

____#,   ____♭,   ____♮

5. "How looney are you? YIKES! Don't answer that question!! How tooney are you? Why not be both and play this looney tooney this afternooney AS FAST AS YOU CAN!!! That's all, folks!"

That's the Way It Is

Words and Music by
Max Martin, Kristian Lundin, and Andress Carlsson

Moderately

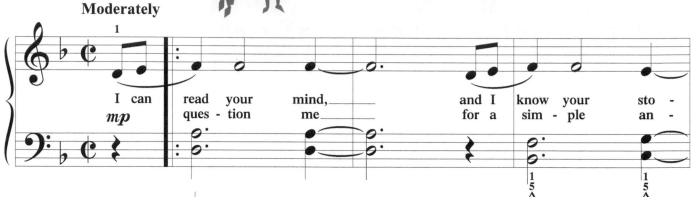

I can read your mind, and I know your sto -
ques - tion me for a sim - ple an -

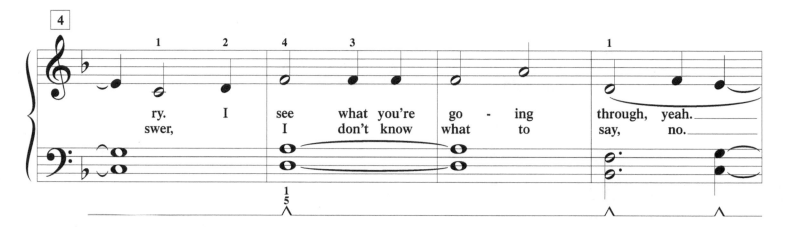

ry. I see what you're go - ing through, yeah.
swer, I don't know what to say, no.

It's an up - hill climb, and I'm feel - ing sor -
But it's plain to see, if you stick to - geth -

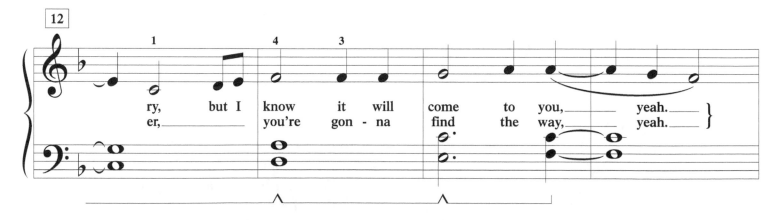

ry, but I know it will come to you, yeah.
er, you're gon - na find the way, yeah.

FF1260

Don't sur - ren - der,_____ 'cause you can win_____ in this thing called_____ love.

When you want it the most,_____ there's no eas - y way out._____ When you're read - y to go_____ and your heart's left in doubt,_____ don't give

DISCOVERY Write the letter names of the chords that are played over and over from *measures 25 to 36*.

_____, _____, _____, and _____

¢ = $\frac{2}{2}$ —two beats per measure
—the half note receives one beat

- Write **1 + 2 +** (1 and 2 and) under the correct beats for each measure below.

- Then play the melody at a moderate tempo. Count aloud, "1 and 2 and."

That's the Way It Is

Words and Music by
Max Martin, Kristian Lundin, and Andress Carlsson

Rhythm Challenge: Play the melody above with the metronome ticking at ♩ = 80. Feel **two beats** per measure. Can you accurately follow the beat of the metronome?

Seventh (7th)

The interval of a **7th** covers 7 keys and 7 letter names. On the staff, a 7th is: **line to line** or **space to space**.

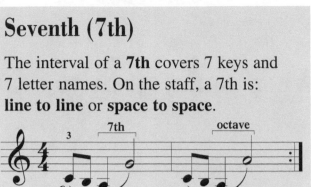

I Swear

Words and Music by
Gary Baker and Frank J. Myers

Lyrics within the music:

I see the ques-tions in your eyes. I know what's weigh-ing on your mind. But you can be sure I know my part. 'Cause I'll

FF1260

like a shad - ow that's by___ your___ side, I'll be there.___

For bet - ter or worse, till death do us part, I'll

love you with ev - er - y beat of my heart,___ I swear,___ I swear,___

I swear.___ rit.

DISCOVERY Which two measures use this R.H. rhythm? $\frac{4}{4}$ ♩♩♩ ♩. ♪ *measures* ____ and ____
Write **1 2 3 4** under the beats of these measures.
Then tap or clap the rhythm for your teacher.

FF1260

"...by the moon and the stars"

A lead sheet is the *melody only*, with chord symbols written above to show the harmony.

1. First play the melody alone with your R.H.

2. Then add *blocked chords* with your L.H. as shown by the chord symbols.* Play two chords per measure, on **beats 1** and **3**. (You may wish to draw arrows to show beats 1 and 3 in each measure.)

I Swear

Key of C Major

Words and Music by
Gary Baker and Frank J. Myers

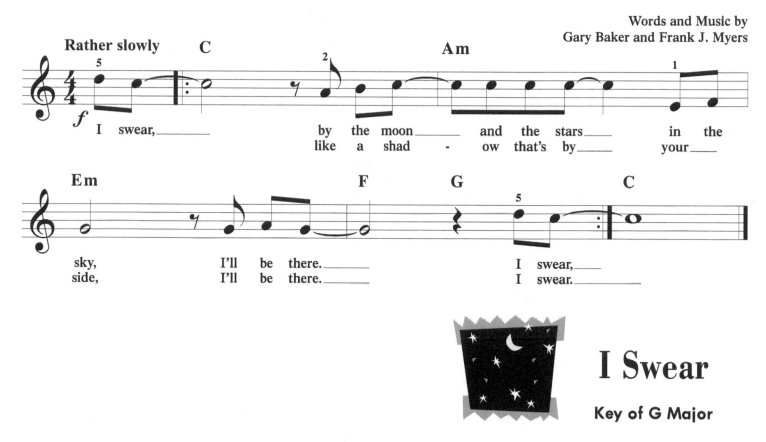

I Swear

Key of G Major

Words and Music by
Gary Baker and Frank J. Myers

*Teacher Note: The student may play all chords in root position.

6 —six beats in a measure, grouped as 3+3 (♪♪♪ + ♪♪♪)
8 —the 8th note receives one beat

For faster tempos, **6/8** is felt with two pulses per measure,
the ♩. getting the beat.

Superman
(Theme)

John Williams

Lively March tempo, "in two"

FF1260

DISCOVERY Circle the *time signature change* to $\frac{4}{4}$. Where does it return to $\frac{6}{8}$?

Super six-eight

For each rhythm below:

- Write the counts **1 2 3 4 5 6** under the correct beats in each measure.

- Indicate *two* pulses per measure by drawing arrows as shown in the example.

Quickly, "in two"

a.

With energy, "in two"

measure 1–4

b.

Bright March tempo, "in two"

measures 29–32

c.

Quickly, "in two"

measures 37–40

d.

- Play each rhythm above *hands together* on **C's**. (Use finger 3 in each hand.)
  Play at a fast tempo, feeling **two pulses** per measure.

From a Distance

Inner Ledger Notes

Ledger lines are short lines used to extend the staff. Play these notes on the piano, saying the note names aloud.

Warm-up:

Lyrics and Music by
Julie Gold

Moderately slowly

mf

mp

From a dis - tance, the world looks blue____ and green ____ and the snow - capped ____ moun - tains white.

From a dis - tance, the o - cean meets ____ the stream

FF12

and the ea - gle takes to flight.

From a dis - tance, there is har - mo - ny,

and it ech - oes through the land.

It's the voice of hope; it's the voice of peace;

it's the voice of ev - 'ry man.

DISCOVERY On what beat does this piece begin?

". . .from a distance, there is harmony"

Complete the information for each musical example.

From a Distance

1. Name the **intervals** in the boxes below the notes.

Lyrics and Music by
Julie Gold

Intervals: 3rd

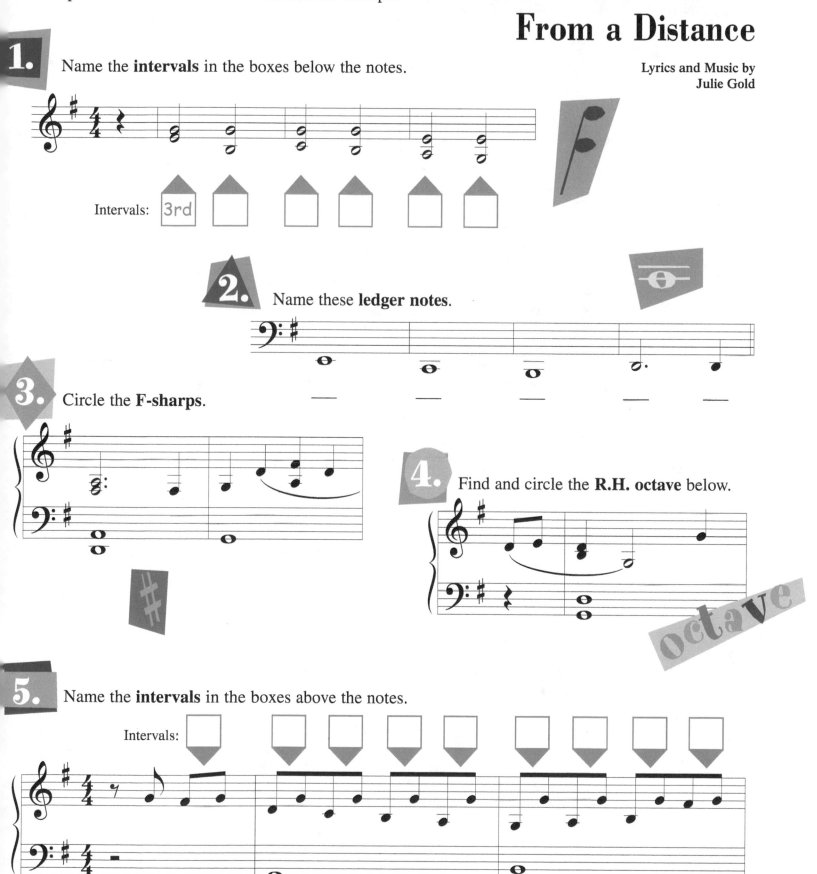

2. Name these **ledger notes**.

3. Circle the **F-sharps**.

4. Find and circle the **R.H. octave** below.

5. Name the **intervals** in the boxes above the notes.

Intervals:

The Pink Panther

Music by Henry Mancini

Swing Rhythm (common in jazz and blues)

If the **tempo mark** includes the word "swing," play the 8th notes with a *long-short* swing rhythm.

Tap (or clap) and say:

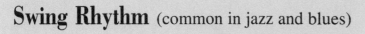

long short long short long short long short

DISCOVERY What interval is played most often throughout *measures 1–8*?

FF1

Panther Swing

Review: Swing Rhythm

In *swing rhythm*, 8th notes are played in a *long-short* pattern.

l-o-n-g short l-o-n-g short

Your teacher will play either example **a** or **b**. Notice the tempo marks:

Moderately, *no swing* (on the left)   **Moderately, *with swing*** (on the right)

Listen for *straight* 8th notes or 8th notes in *swing rhythm*. Circle the example you hear.

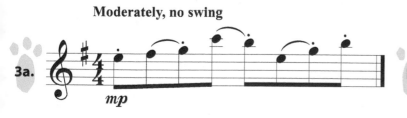

260

31

I Will Always Love You

Words and Music by Dolly Parton

Key Signature for D Major

F# and C#

Warm-up: I IV I

Rather slowly

1. If I should stay, I would

2. 3. *See additional lyrics*

on - ly be in your way. So I'll go, but I

know I'll think of you ev - 'ry step of the way. And

Chorus

I will al-ways love you. I

Additional Lyrics

2. Bittersweet memories
   That is all I'm taking with me.
   So, goodbye, please don't cry.
   We both know I'm not what you need.
   To Chorus

3. I hope life treats you kind
   And I hope you have all you've dreamed of.
   I wish you joy and happiness.
   But above all this, I wish you love.
   To Chorus

 DISCOVERY Play a **I** and **IV chord** in the key of D major.

Then circle five IV chords for the L.H. in this arrangement.

I Will Always Count

The ♪ ♩ ♪ rhythm is common in popular, ragtime, and Latin music.

Tap (or clap) the following rhythm several times. Count aloud.

Count: **1 + 2 + 3 + 4 +**

1. Each rhythm below uses the ♪ ♩ ♪ pattern. Circle the ♪ ♩ ♪ pattern each time it appears. Then write **1 + 2 + 3 + 4 +** (1 and 2 and 3 and 4 and) under the notes in each box.

Play on a **D major chord**

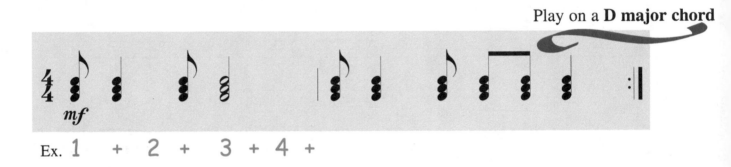

Ex. 1 + 2 + 3 + 4 +

Play on a **D minor chord**

Play on an **A major chord**

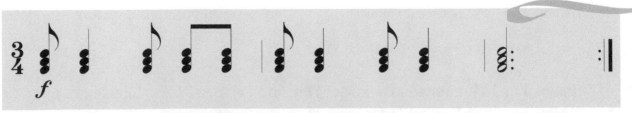

FF1

2. Circle the ♪ ♩ ♪ pattern each time it occurs in this D major scale. Play hands
separately, then hands together. (Your teacher may ask you to count aloud.)

Extra Credit: Transpose to **C major** and **G major**.

3. Circle the ♪ ♩ ♪ pattern each time it occurs with these I and IV chords.
Then play. (Your teacher may ask you to count aloud.)

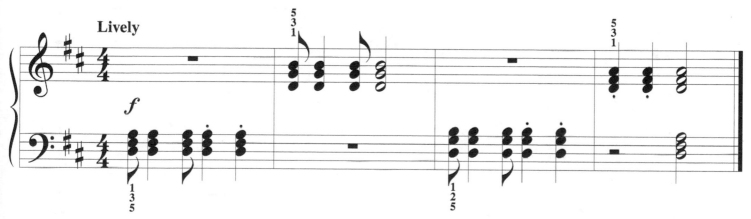

Extra Credit: Transpose to **F major** and **G major**.

4. Circle the ♪ ♩ ♪ pattern each time it occurs in the L.H. accompaniment.
Then play. (Your teacher may ask you to count aloud.)

Extra Credit: Transpose to **A major** and **C major**.

One-Octave Arpeggio

Arpeggio—the notes of a chord played up or down the keyboard. To play a *one-hand arpeggio*, extend the hand over the keys.

F major warm-up:

Animaniacs
(Main Title Theme)

Lyrics by
Paul Ruegger

Music by
Richard Stone

FF1

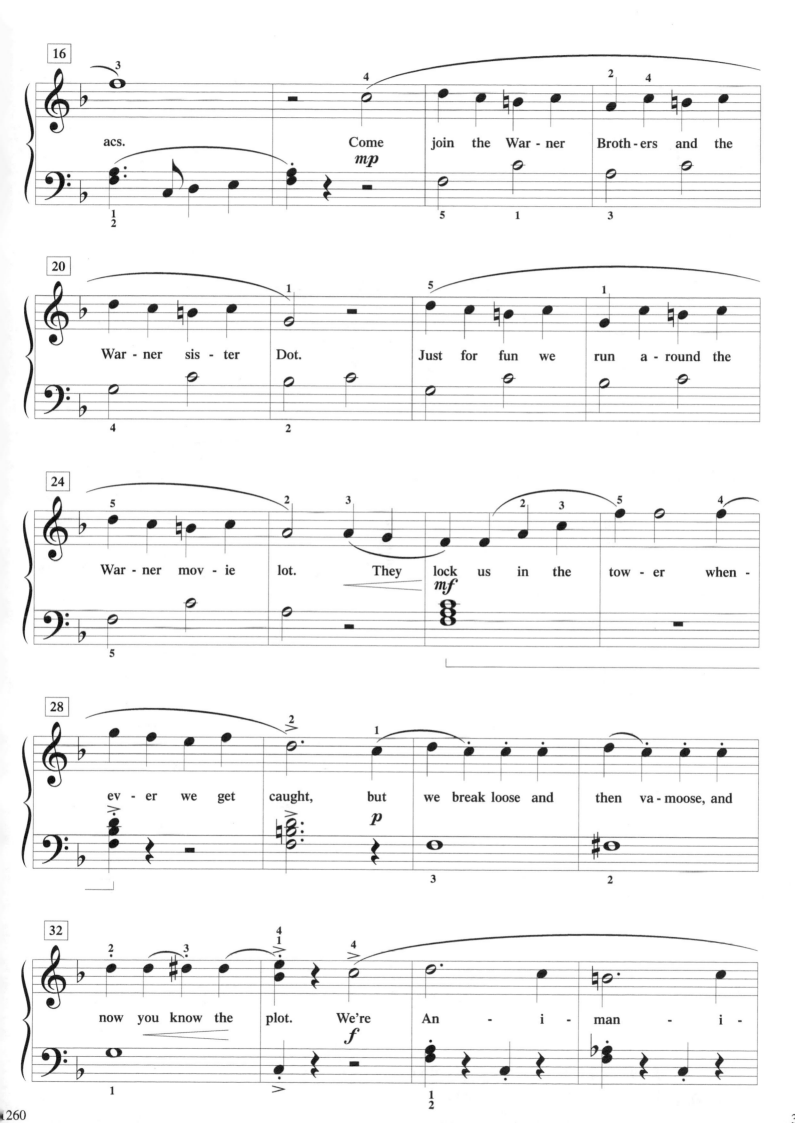

DISCOVERY An **F major one-octave arpeggio** occurs three times in this arrangement.
Point out each time it appears.

"...zany to the max"

Animaniacs
(Main Title Theme)

Music by Richard Stone
Lyrics by Paul Ruegger

The Alberti bass accompaniment uses this pattern for the notes of a chord: *bottom top middle top*

- Play the example below, noticing this pattern.

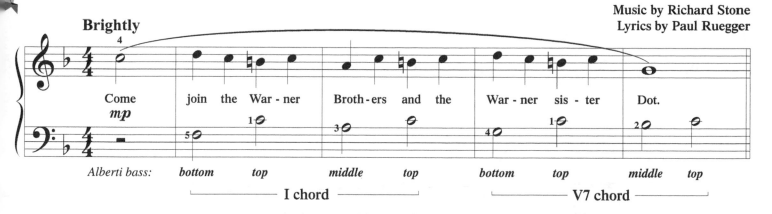

Brightly

Come join the War-ner Broth-ers and the War-ner sis-ter Dot.
mp

Alberti bass: *bottom top middle top bottom top middle top*

I chord — V7 chord

- Complete the *Alberti bass* patterns by writing the **missing chord tone** above each arrow. (Remember: *bottom top middle top*)

Brightly

Key of ___ Major

Come join the War-ner Broth-ers and the War-ner sis-ter Dot.
mp

I chord — V7 chord

Brightly

Key of ___ Major

Come join the War-ner Broth-ers and the War-ner sis-ter Dot.
mp

I chord — V7 chord

Zany Challenge: For fun, play the musical examples above with these variations:

- R.H. one octave *higher*, L.H. one octave *lower*
- R.H. *staccato*, L.H. *legato*
- **Both hands** as high as possible on the keyboard

MUSIC DICTIONARY

pp	*p*	*mp*	*mf*	*f*	*ff*
pianissimo	*piano*	*mezzo piano*	*mezzo forte*	*forte*	*fortissimo*
very soft	soft	medium soft	medium loud	loud	very loud

crescendo (cresc.)
Play gradually louder.

diminuendo (dim.) or decrescendo (decresc.)
Play gradually softer.

SIGN	TERM	DEFINITION
	accent mark	Play this note louder.
	accidental	A sharp or flat that is not in the key signature. A natural is also an accidental.
	accompaniment	The harmony and rhythm that accompany the melody.
	Alberti bass	A left-hand accompaniment that outlines the notes of a chord using the pattern: *bottom-top-middle-top*.
	arpeggio	The notes of a chord played up or down the keyboard.
	a tempo	Return to the beginning tempo (speed).
	blocked chord	The notes of a chord played together.
	broken chord	The notes of a chord played separately.
	chord	Three or more notes sounding together.
	chord analysis	Naming the chord letter names (Ex. Dm) or the Roman numerals (Ex. I, IV, V7, etc.) of a piece.
	chord symbol	The letter name of the chord indicated above the music. A lower-case "m" is used to show minor.
	chord tone	One of the notes of a chord.
	chorus	A repeated section (music and lyrics) of a popular piece that often features the words of the title.
	chromatic scale	A 12-note scale composed only of half steps.
C	**common time**	$\frac{4}{4}$ time.
₵	**cut time (alla breve)**	Short for $\frac{2}{2}$ time signature. The half note gets the beat. (Two half-note beats per measure.)
	dynamics	The "louds and softs" of music. See dynamic marks above.
	fermata	Hold this note longer than its usual value.
♭	**flat**	A flat lowers a note one half step.
	half step	The distance from one key to the very closest key on the keyboard. (Ex. C-C♯ or E-F)
	interval	The distance between two musical tones or keys on the keyboard. For example, 2nd, 3rd, 4th, 5th, octave.

FF1